U.S. Department of
Transportation
**Federal Railroad
Administration**

North Carolina "Sealed Corridor" Phase IV Assessment – Private Crossings

Office of Railroad
Policy and Development
Washington, DC 20590

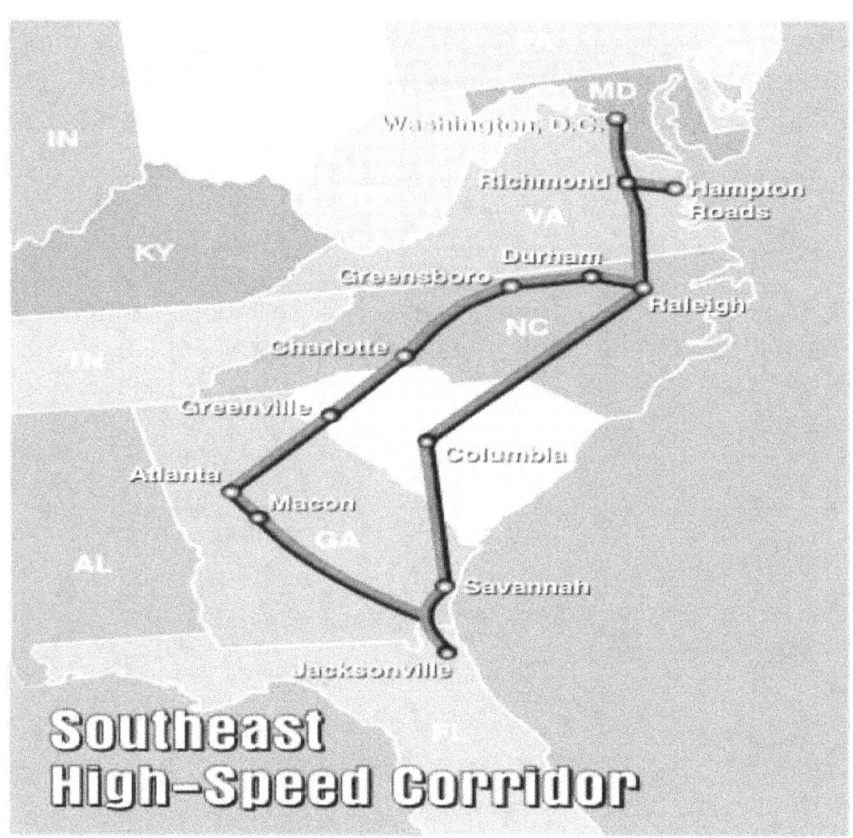

Safety of Highway Railroad Grade Crossings

DOT/FRA/ORD-12/12

Final Report
July 2012

REPORT DOCUMENTATION PAGE

Form Approved
OMB No. 0704-0188

1. AGENCY USE ONLY (Leave blank)	2. REPORT DATE July 2012	3. REPORT TYPE AND DATES COVERED Technical Report October 2008 – February 2010

4. TITLE AND SUBTITLE	5. FUNDING NUMBERS
North Carolina "Sealed Corridor" Phase IV Assessment – Private Crossings	RR97A1/FG277 RR97A2/FG348
6. AUTHOR(S) Patrick Bien-Aime, Anya A. Carroll, and Marco daSilva	

7. PERFORMING ORGANIZATION NAME(S) AND ADDRESS(ES) U.S. Department of Transportation Research and Innovative Technology Administration John A. Volpe National Transportation Systems Center Cambridge, MA 02142	8. PERFORMING ORGANIZATION REPORT NUMBER DOT-VNTSC-FRA-09-14

9. SPONSORING/MONITORING AGENCY NAME(S) AND ADDRESS(ES) U.S. Department of Transportation Federal Railroad Administration Office of Railroad Policy and Development 1200 New Jersey Avenue SE Washington, DC 20590	10. SPONSORING/MONITORING AGENCY REPORT NUMBER DOT/FRA/ORD-12/12

11. SUPPLEMENTARY NOTES
Safety of Highway-Railroad Grade Crossings series Program Manager: Tarek Omar, D.Sc.

12a. DISTRIBUTION/AVAILABILITY STATEMENT This document is available to the public through the FRA Web site at http://www.fra.dot.gov	12b. DISTRIBUTION CODE

13. ABSTRACT (Maximum 200 words)

The U.S. Department of Transportation's (USDOT) Federal Railroad Administration tasked the USDOT Research and Innovative Technology Administration's John A. Volpe National Transportation Systems Center to document the success of the safety improvements at private highway-rail grade crossings along the Charlotte to Raleigh portion of the Southeast High-Speed Rail (SEHSR) Corridor. This set of safety improvements, implemented during Phase IV of North Carolina Department of Transportation's (NCDOT) Sealed Corridor project, targeted the private crossings along that segment of the SEHSR corridor. The Sealed Corridor program aimed at improving or consolidating every highway-rail grade crossing, public and private, along the Charlotte to Raleigh rail route. The research on the Sealed Corridor private crossings, conducted from October 2008 to February 2010, assessed the progress made at the 44 crossings between Charlotte and Raleigh that have been treated with improved warning devices or closed from 1990 through 2008. Two approaches were used to describe benefits in terms of lives saved: a fatal crash analysis to derive estimated lives saved and prediction of lives saved based on the reduction of risk at the treated crossings. Both methods estimated that over 1.5 lives have been potentially saved at private crossings as a result of the 44 improvements implemented through 2008. Analysis also shows that the resulting reduction in incidents, as a result of the crossing improvements, is sustainable through 2010, when anticipated exposure and train speeds along the corridor will increase.

14. SUBJECT TERMS Accident reduction, alternative safety measures, education and enforcement, highway-rail intersections, safety, video data, violation reduction, high-speed rail, risk assessment, private crossings	15. NUMBER OF PAGES 49
	16. PRICE CODE

17. SECURITY CLASSIFICATION OF REPORT Unclassified	18. SECURITY CLASSIFICATION OF THIS PAGE Unclassified	19. SECURITY CLASSIFICATION OF ABSTRACT Unclassified	20. LIMITATION OF ABSTRACT

i

METRIC/ENGLISH CONVERSION FACTORS

ENGLISH TO METRIC	METRIC TO ENGLISH
LENGTH (APPROXIMATE)	**LENGTH** (APPROXIMATE)
1 inch (in) = 2.5 centimeters (cm)	1 millimeter (mm) = 0.04 inch (in)
1 foot (ft) = 30 centimeters (cm)	1 centimeter (cm) = 0.4 inch (in)
1 yard (yd) = 0.9 meter (m)	1 meter (m) = 3.3 feet (ft)
1 mile (mi) = 1.6 kilometers (km)	1 meter (m) = 1.1 yards (yd)
	1 kilometer (km) = 0.6 mile (mi)
AREA (APPROXIMATE)	**AREA** (APPROXIMATE)
1 square inch (sq in, in^2) = 6.5 square centimeters (cm^2)	1 square centimeter (cm^2) = 0.16 square inch (sq in, in^2)
1 square foot (sq ft, ft^2) = 0.09 square meter (m^2)	1 square meter (m^2) = 1.2 square yards (sq yd, yd^2)
1 square yard (sq yd, yd^2) = 0.8 square meter (m^2)	1 square kilometer (km^2) = 0.4 square mile (sq mi, mi^2)
1 square mile (sq mi, mi^2) = 2.6 square kilometers (km^2)	10,000 square meters (m^2) = 1 hectare (ha) = 2.5 acres
1 acre = 0.4 hectare (he) = 4,000 square meters (m^2)	
MASS - WEIGHT (APPROXIMATE)	**MASS - WEIGHT** (APPROXIMATE)
1 ounce (oz) = 28 grams (gm)	1 gram (gm) = 0.036 ounce (oz)
1 pound (lb) = 0.45 kilogram (kg)	1 kilogram (kg) = 2.2 pounds (lb)
1 short ton = 2,000 pounds (lb) = 0.9 tonne (t)	1 tonne (t) = 1,000 kilograms (kg) = 1.1 short tons
VOLUME (APPROXIMATE)	**VOLUME** (APPROXIMATE)
1 teaspoon (tsp) = 5 milliliters (ml)	1 milliliter (ml) = 0.03 fluid ounce (fl oz)
1 tablespoon (tbsp) = 15 milliliters (ml)	1 liter (l) = 2.1 pints (pt)
1 fluid ounce (fl oz) = 30 milliliters (ml)	1 liter (l) = 1.06 quarts (qt)
1 cup (c) = 0.24 liter (l)	1 liter (l) = 0.26 gallon (gal)
1 pint (pt) = 0.47 liter (l)	
1 quart (qt) = 0.96 liter (l)	
1 gallon (gal) = 3.8 liters (l)	
1 cubic foot (cu ft, ft^3) = 0.03 cubic meter (m^3)	1 cubic meter (m^3) = 36 cubic feet (cu ft, ft^3)
1 cubic yard (cu yd, yd^3) = 0.76 cubic meter (m^3)	1 cubic meter (m^3) = 1.3 cubic yards (cu yd, yd^3)
TEMPERATURE (EXACT)	**TEMPERATURE** (EXACT)
[(x-32)(5/9)] °F = y °C	[(9/5) y + 32] °C = x °F

QUICK INCH - CENTIMETER LENGTH CONVERSION

QUICK FAHRENHEIT - CELSIUS TEMPERATURE CONVERSIO

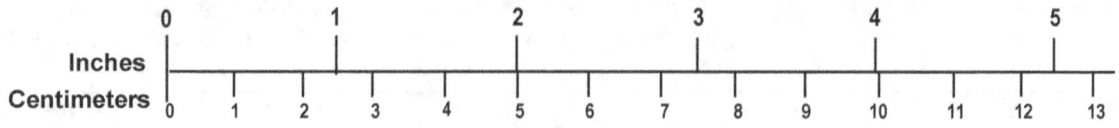

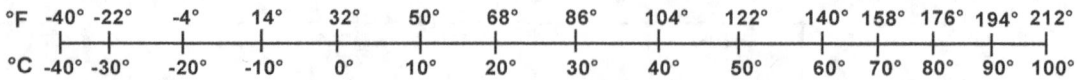

For more exact and or other conversion factors, see NIST Miscellaneous Publication 286, Units of Weights and Measures. Price $2.50 SD Catalog No. C13 10286

Updated 6/17/98

Acknowledgments

The U.S. Department of Transportation (USDOT) Federal Railroad Administration (FRA) Office of Research and Development sponsored the work leading to this report. The authors would like to thank Sam Alibrahim P.E. (Professional Engineer), Chief of the Signals, Train Control, and Communications Division, FRA; and Leonard Allen, Program Manager, Signals, Train Control, and Communications Division, FRA, for their guidance and direction in developing this report.

Tashi Ngamdung, Systems Engineering and Safety Division, USDOT Research and Innovative Technology Administration's John A. Volpe National Transportation Systems (Volpe Center), provided support in data collection, modeling, and report preparation. The authors would also like to acknowledge John McGuiggin, P.E., Chief of the Systems Engineering and Safety Division, Volpe Center, for his leadership and direction.

Special thanks are given the North Carolina Department of Transportation's Rail Division for their assistance in data collection and input for this report, as well as Paul Worley and Andrew Thomas.

Contents

Illustrations

Tables

Executive Summary

This research, conducted from October 2008 to February 2010, assesses the potential safety benefits provided by the safety improvements at private highway-rail grade crossings in North Carolina along the Charlotte to Raleigh portion of the Southeast High-Speed Rail Corridor (SEHSR). The North Carolina Department of Transportation (NCDOT) proceeded with this set of safety improvements, commonly grouped under the program entitled Private Crossing Safety Initiative (PCSI), under Phase IV of its Sealed Corridor program. The progress is described in terms of safety benefits. Crash data through 2008 were examined to ensure any incidents that may have occurred at crossings improved through September 2008 would be included. This report also contains an analysis and evaluation of whether the resulting reduction in incidents is sustainable through 2010 when train speeds along the corridor could achieve 110 miles per hour (mph), although discussions with NCDOT rail staff indicate train speeds may only increase to 79 mph. Therefore, an evaluation of five different rail speed variables—No Build (110 mph in 2010), No Build (79 mph in 2010), Full Build (110 mph in 2010), Full Build (79 mph in 2010), and Full Build without any rail speed increase in 2010—were analyzed and compared.

Safety benefits are developed through the use of two methods: a fatal crash analysis approach to estimate lives saved through 2008, and a prediction of lives saved based on the reduction of risk at those treated crossings using a modified USDOT Accident Prediction Formula (APF) (10, 11, 12). The resulting risk reduction that can be anticipated through 2010 is calculated at operating train speeds of 110 mph along the corridor.

The NCDOT PCSI activity encompasses 46 private crossings between Charlotte and Raleigh, NC. As of September 2008, a total of 44 of the 46 crossings have been improved or closed. The research documented in this report calculates the estimated number of lives saved based on the improvements made to these highway-rail intersections from 1990 to September 2008. The results of this research provide a substantive analysis of the Sealed Corridor private crossing implementation and provide Federal, State, and local organizations a successful model to use on future high-speed rail corridors.

Section 3 shows the analysis and results of Phase IV private crossings and Phase I–III public crossings. Table 1 shows the effectiveness rate used on the treatment types utilized above the standard two-quadrant gate system.

Table 1. Effectiveness of Crossing Improvements

	Closure	Traffic Channelization Devices	Four-Quadrant Gates only, No Presence Detection	Four-Quadrant Gates with Channelization	Grade Separation
Effectiveness*	100%	75%	82%	92%	100%

* Effectiveness over standard gates in reducing crashes from the FRA Train Horn Final Rule (13).

In addition, the following assumptions were made for other implemented upgrades of passive crossings along the Sealed Corridor:

- The effectiveness rate for untreated crossings was assumed to be zero;

- A stop sign effectiveness of 35 percent over passive crossings was assumed based on the current literature (14);

- Gates with locking mechanisms were assumed to be as effective as a standard two-quadrant gate system, which is 78 percent more effective than passive crossings (10); and

- Closure of crossings assumed an effectiveness of 100 percent over passive crossings, the risk at a closed crossing is reduced to zero.

Conclusions

At least one and a half lives have been potentially saved.

The fatal crash analysis method was used to calculate the differences between the annual (or monthly) fatality rates, based on actual experience at the improved crossings, before and after the improvements were made at each crossing. To calculate lives saved, those differences were multiplied by the number of years (or months) occurring between 1990 and September 2008, the period during which each of the respective improvements was made. The sum of these results was then calculated over all of the crossings that were improved. This resulted in an estimate of 1.5 lives saved as a result of the 44 improvements implemented over the approximately 18-year period.

The study also used the modified USDOT APF and severity formulas, which recognize the probabilistic nature of grade crossing fatalities and rely on a combination of actual experience at the improved crossings and a database of experience at similar crossings nationwide, to estimate the annual fatality rates at each private crossing before and after improvements were implemented. Those numbers were summed to determine the corridor-wide results. This method estimated that the improvements implemented through September 2008 would reduce fatalities by approximately 0.39 each year. This analysis predicted a larger number of lives saved compared with the fatal crash analysis results. This may be because the APF method incorporates more variables, such as train and vehicle traffic, and addresses the crossing environment risk.

The estimated accident reduction result is sustainable.

To estimate future incident reduction rates, the second of the above methods was used to ensure that increases in train and vehicle exposure over time were considered in the analysis. It was estimated by NCDOT that the vehicular traffic volume and the frequency and speed of trains will increase by the year 2010. The second method is capable of taking those factors into account.

Figure 1 shows the estimated annual fatalities under two conditions: all 46 private crossings have been treated (Full Build), and no improvements were implemented on the 46 private crossings (No Build). The graph shows a decrease in risk from 1994 to 1998, followed by an increase in risk with the introduction of the higher train frequency and speed. The graph shows the influence of the improvements, which were initiated in 2002, on reducing the annual fatalities through 2010. The improvements at the remaining two private crossings in the corridor were assumed to be implemented in 2009. The gradual increase in traffic volume and train frequency from 2008 through 2010 is expected to increase annual fatalities under all conditions. Finally, the increase in train speed to 110 mph assumed to occur in 2010 would further increase all fatality rates calculated.

As can be seen in Figure 1, the difference in annual fatalities (the number of lives saved per year) under all conditions (Full Build and No Build) would continue to increase through 2010. By 2010, the fatality rate at private crossings resulting from the full implementation of Phase IV of the Sealed Corridor would be 44 percent lower than if no implementation were executed and train speed increased to 110 mph. Further analysis indicates that the fatality rate would be 42.8 percent lower if the speed increased to only 79 mph in 2010, and 40.4 percent lower with no increase in speed in 2010. Discussions with NCDOT Rail Division staff indicated train speeds may only increase to 79 mph in 2010. Therefore, it is estimated that approximately 43 percent of the risk at private crossings could be eliminated along the corridor.

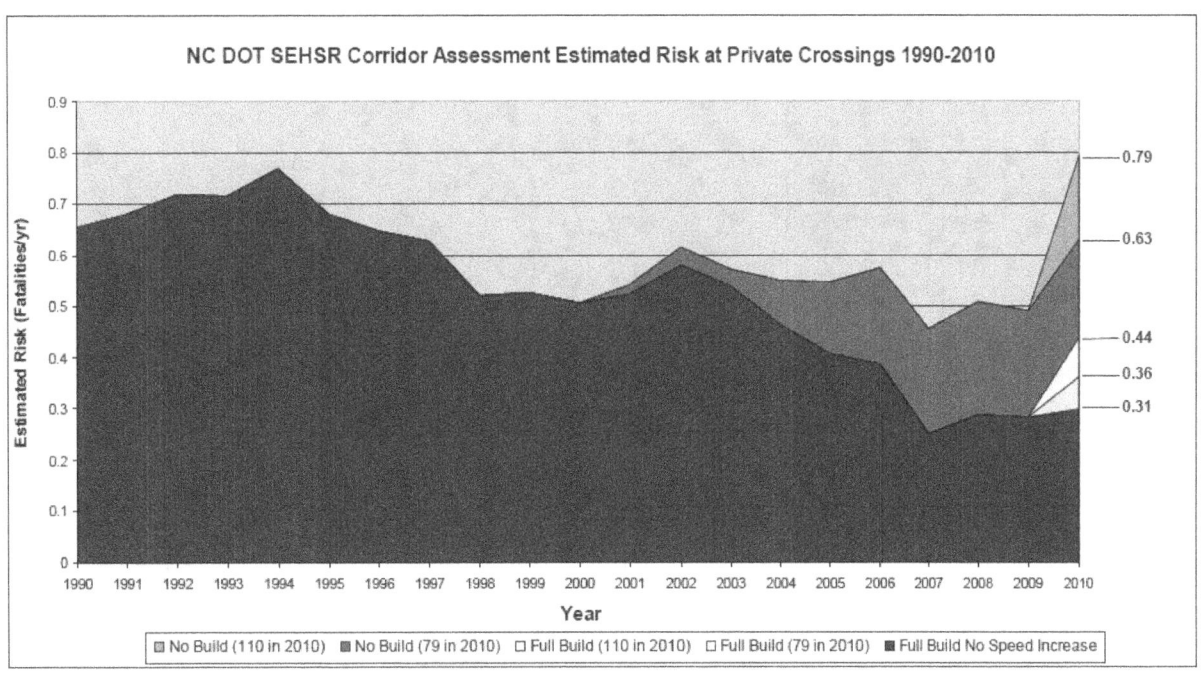

Figure 1. NCDOT SEHSR Corridor Estimated Risk at Private Crossings 1990–2010

Phases I–III (Public Crossings) and Phase IV (Private Crossings) Results
Given the estimated risk through 2010 on the entire NCDOT corridor, including public crossings that were treated during Phases I–III of the program and with the assumption of railroad operational speed increases to 110 mph, the No Build condition shows an increase in risk of 3.2

fatalities per year more than the 2010 Full Build condition. If speeds were increased to only 79 mph, the No Build condition shows an increase in risk of 2.8 fatalities per year more than the Full Build. Further analysis indicates an increase of 1.8 fatalities per year more than the 2010 Full Build condition if there were no train speed increases. By 2010, the fatality rate resulting from the full implementation of all the public and private crossing treatments along the entire NCDOT corridor would be 52 percent lower than if no implementation were executed and the train speed increased to 110 mph. The fatality rate would be 50.9 percent lower if the train speeds increase to only 79 mph in 2010, and 46.5 percent lower with no increase in train speed in 2010. This risk assessment illustrates that the treatments made by the NCDOT Sealed Corridor program at all public and private crossings have resulted in additional benefits in terms of lives saved through 2010 and will save even more lives for years thereafter.

1. Introduction

1.1 Background

Private highway-rail grade crossing safety has been a matter of concern to both the U.S. Department of Transportation (USDOT) and the National Transportation Safety Board (NTSB) for more than two decades. The USDOT's Federal Railroad Administration (FRA) hosted an open meeting on July 13, 1993, to initiate an industry-wide discussion concerning private crossing safety. Since then, both the USDOT and NTSB have publicly weighed in on the topic. The 1994 USDOT Rail-Highway Crossing Safety Action Plan addressed the need to review safety concerns at private highway-rail grade crossings (1). In the 2004 USDOT Highway-Rail Crossing Safety and Trespass Prevention Action Plan (2), the department committed to lead an effort to define responsibility for safety at private highway-rail grade crossings.

Private highway-rail grade crossings are not maintained by public authority and are found on roadways not open to public use. According to the USDOT National Highway-Rail Crossing Inventory maintained by FRA, over 85,100 private crossings existed in the United States as of 2008 (3). Typical types of private crossings include the following:

- Farm crossings that provide access between tracts of land lying across a railroad right-of-way;
- Industrial plant crossings that provide access between plant facilities across a railroad right-of-way;
- Residential access crossings over which the occupants and their invitees reach private residences from another road, frequently a public road parallel and adjacent to the railroad right-of-way;
- Temporary crossings established for the duration of a private construction project or other seasonal activity across a railroad right-of-way (4).

The USDOT Federal Highway Administration's (FHWA) *Manual on Uniform Traffic Control Devices for Streets and Highways* (MUTCD) 2003 edition (5) defines a public roadway as any road or street under the jurisdiction of and maintained by a public agency and open to public travel. If either approach to a crossing does not qualify as a public roadway, then the crossing is typically classified as a private crossing.

Private highway-rail grade crossings may be governed by legal agreements between private property owners and private railroad companies. Currently, few Federal regulations pertain to the safety, operation, maintenance, or responsibility designations at private highway-rail grade crossings, although some States and local jurisdictions have assumed varying degrees of authority over them.

The North Carolina Department of Transportation (NCDOT) plays a prominent role among States pursuing High-Speed Ground Transportation (HSGT) development. The Southeast High-Speed Rail (SEHSR) Corridor is anticipated to connect Washington, DC, through Richmond, VA, to Raleigh and Charlotte, NC, with extensions south to Columbia, SC, Savannah, GA, and southwest to Greenville, SC, Atlanta and Macon, GA, and Jacksonville, FL. Recognizing that improved safety accompanies improved service, the State has instituted an innovative Sealed Corridor program initiative, which aims to improve or consolidate every highway-rail grade crossing, public and private, along the Charlotte to Raleigh rail route. The multiyear grade crossing improvements were funded through the Next Generation High-Speed Rail and Section 1103(c) programs (8). Private crossings cannot receive Federal Section 130 funds for improvements.

The NCDOT Sealed Corridor improvements were implemented in four phases. Phases I, II, and III consisted of closing or improving 189 public crossings. The Volpe National Transportation Systems Center (Volpe Center) performed an assessment of Phases I, II, and III in earlier studies and reported their findings in a Report to Congress (8) and an FRA technical report (9). Phase IV consisted of closing private crossings where feasible and improving others with cross bucks, stop signs, automatic flashing lights and gates, and gates with locking mechanisms.

Approximately 400 incidents, resulting in over 30 fatalities, occur at private highway-rail grade crossings nationwide per year. Historically, the number of fatalities at private crossings has exceeded the total number of on-duty deaths among railroad employees in all rail operations. Over the past two decades, the number of incidents at public highway-rail grade crossings has decreased by approximately 60 percent, whereas the number of incidents at private crossings has decreased only by approximately 26 percent (7).

Many safety treatments and initiatives have been implemented at public crossings using both public and private funding. The steep decline in incidents at public crossings is likely associated with those implementations. However, because of the characteristics of and the inherent responsibilities regarding private property, private crossings have not received many of the public grade crossing treatments and initiatives.

Private highway-rail grade crossings have been a matter of concern to USDOT, private industry, and the general public for almost two decades. Not all items of concern can be addressed immediately because of time and budget constraints; however, multiple agencies within the USDOT are involved in the effort. In particular, FRA and FHWA have taken initiatives to advance the safety of private highway-rail grade crossings.

The FHWA Manual on Uniform Traffic Control Devices (MUTCD) defines a public highway-rail grade crossing as any intersection between a public roadway and railroad (5). The roadway on either side of the crossing must be a public roadway (i.e., open to public travel and under the jurisdiction of, and maintained by, a public authority). If either approach to a crossing does not qualify as a public roadway, then the crossing is typically classified as private.

In 2006, more than 94,400 private highway-rail grade crossings were in existence in the United States; 400 incidents, resulting in over 30 fatalities, occurred at a number of these crossings (7).

Currently, accurate estimates of the physical conditions, operations and maintenance procedures, and estimated risks at private highway-rail grade crossings in the United States are unavailable, in large part because private crossing data are limited, incomplete, and, in some instances, inaccurate. Furthermore, the nature of private ownership and the contractual rights between private property owners and railroads have complicated Federal, State, and local governmental authority over these types of crossings.

From July 2006 through July 2007, FRA, with support from the USDOT's Research and Innovative Technology Administration (RITA) and Volpe Center, conducted a safety inquiry to solicit comments from private crossing owners, railroads, and other stakeholder parties on safety issues at private highway-rail grade crossings. This report, entitled *Private Highway-Rail Grade Crossing Safety Research and Inquiry* (6), documented the information gathered during the safety inquiry. The document included the process employed by FRA and Volpe Center, written and oral commentary, and a summary of regional and local regulations, standards, and methodological and operational practices specific to private crossings.

This research, conducted from October 2008 to February 2010, reviews NCDOT's fourth phase of implementation of warning devices and/or consolidation of highway-rail grade crossings along the North Carolina section of the SEHSR Sealed Corridor with regard to private crossings. This assessment is the third in a series of research studies conducted on the effectiveness of treatments along the corridor. The first two studies contained assessments of improvements implemented during Phases I, II, and III to public crossings along the corridor through North Carolina. These assessments are contained in a report to Congress (8) and an FRA technical report (9).

The report is organized into five sections. Section 1 describes the North Carolina Sealed Corridor, defines the treatment types, and lists crossings by upgrade. Section 2 describes the crash analysis method used and summarizes the subset of four private crossings within Phase IV that had fatal crashes. The analysis details the findings concerning pretreatment fatalities and the post-improvement lives saved over all 46 private crossings along the NCDOT Sealed Corridor. Section 2 also describes the modified USDOT APF (10–12), the assumptions used within the formula, and the results calculated through 2008. Section 3 presents the results of the entire North Carolina portion of the Sealed Corridor, including the previous analysis of the public crossing improvements done during Phase I, II, and III. Section 4 presents the findings and conclusions of the assessment of the NCDOT Sealed Corridor Phase IV improvements.

1.2   NCDOT Sealed Corridor Background

North Carolina plays an important role among States pursuing HSGT development. Part of the SEHSR Corridor is anticipated to connect Washington, DC, through Richmond, VA, to Raleigh and Charlotte, NC, with extensions south to Columbia, SC, Savannah, GA, and southwest to Greenville, SC, Atlanta and Macon, GA, and Jacksonville, FL (see Figure 2). The North Carolina Sealed Corridor architecture is typical of the five originally designated high-speed rail corridors nationwide. The NCDOT corridor is typically single track including sidings and contains approximately one crossing per mile. As of 2003, Norfolk Southern operated approximately 30 freight trains a day on the main line from Charlotte to Greensboro and approximately 20 on the line from Greensboro to Raleigh. In addition, AMTRAK operated six (6) passenger trains a day over the entire line segment. The corridor has a mix of public and private crossings, and the route contains both urban as well as rural environs. The tracks are designated as Class 4, for which the maximum allowable operating speed is 60 mph for freight trains and 80 mph for passenger trains, according to the limits imposed by 49 CFR section 213.9.

Plans for this corridor include increasing the operational speeds to 110 mph for both freight and passenger trains (i.e. upgrading the track to class 6).

Recognizing that enhanced safety measures improve service, the State has instituted an innovative Sealed Corridor initiative, which aims to improve or consolidate every highway-rail grade crossing, public and private, along the Charlotte to Raleigh rail route. The grade crossing improvements were funded through grants from FRA's Next Generation High-Speed Rail and Section 1103c programs (8).

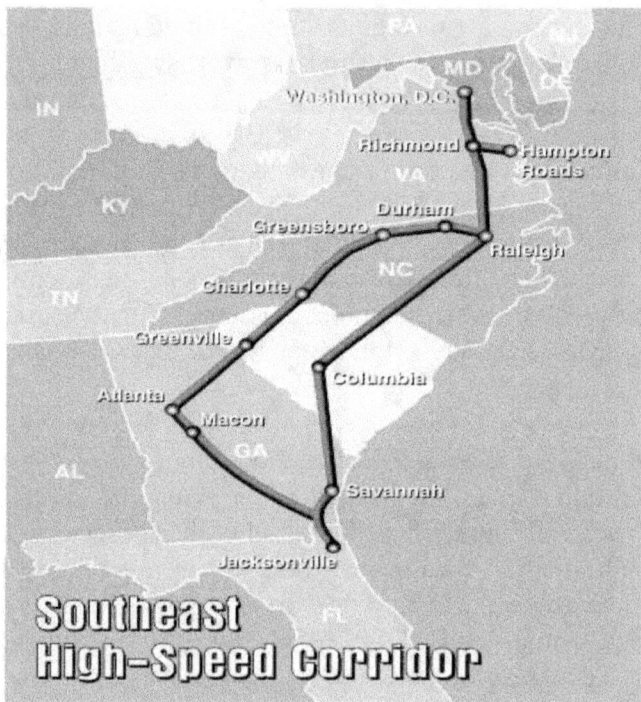

Figure 2. Southeast High-Speed Rail Corridor

The NCDOT Sealed Corridor improvements were implemented in four phases. Phases I, II, and III consisted of closing or improving 189 public crossings. The Volpe Center performed an assessment of Phases I, II, and III in earlier studies and published its findings in a Report to Congress (8) and an FRA technical report (9). Phase IV, otherwise known as the PCSI, consisted of closing or improving private crossings along the route.

1.3 Purpose

The purpose of this research, conducted from October 2008 to February 2010, is to assess the potential benefits provided by the safety improvements at private highway-rail grade crossings in the State of North Carolina along the Charlotte to Raleigh portion of the SEHSR. The NCDOT's Rail Division proceeded with this set of safety improvements, commonly grouped under the PCSI program, under Phase IV of its Sealed Corridor program. Crash data were examined from 1990 through 2008 to ensure the inclusion of all incidents that may have occurred at crossings improved through September 2008. This report also contains an analysis and evaluation of whether the resulting reduction in incidents is sustainable through 2010 when train speeds along the corridor could achieve 110 mph.

Discussions with NCDOT Rail Division's staff indicate train speeds may only increase to 79 mph through 2010. Therefore, five different improvement scenarios and railroad operational speed combinations—(No Build (110 mph in 2010), No Build (79 mph in 2010), Full Build (110 mph in 2010), Full Build (79 mph in 2010), and Full Build without any speed increase in 2010)—were analyzed and compared.

Safety benefits are estimated through the use of two techniques: a fatal crash analysis approach to calculate the potential lives saved through 2008; and a prediction of lives saved based on the reduction of risk at those treated crossings using the modified USDOT APF and severity formulas. The resulting risk reduction that can be anticipated through the year 2010 is calculated at operating train speeds of 110 mph along the corridor.

The PCSI plans to close some of the private crossings along the Sealed Corridor, or install additional warning devices (e.g., cross bucks, stop signs, flashing lights and gates, and gates with locking mechanisms) at the 46 crossings located along that Charlotte to Raleigh, NC, route. As of September 2008, a total of 44 of the 46 crossings have been improved or closed. The research documented in this report calculates the estimated number of lives saved based on the improvements made to these highway-rail intersections from 1990 to September 2008. This research offers a substantive analysis of the Sealed Corridor private crossings improvement initiatives and provides Federal, State, and local organizations a successful model to use for future high-speed rail corridors.

This research also contains an analysis and evaluation of whether the resulting estimated reduction in crashes is sustainable through 2010 when train speeds along the corridor are estimated to achieve 110 mph and all 46 private crossings have been treated or closed.

1.4   Objective

The objectives of this research are twofold:

1. To review variables—number of tracks, number of train movements, and types of warning devices—associated with data fields through careful analyses of various databases, including the FRA Railroad Accident Incident Reporting System (RAIRS), NCDOT collision reports, police reports, and newspaper articles. Using the fatal crash analysis approach, statistical databases were examined to estimate the number of lives saved through 2008 along the NCDOT Sealed Corridor, and

2. To determine, using the modified USDOT APF, whether the treatments at all private crossings provide a sustainable crash reduction condition rate through 2010 when train speeds are projected to increase to as much as 110 mph.

This assessment discusses pretreatment fatalities, estimated pretreatment risk, and post-treatment condition benefits in terms of estimated lives saved. A prediction of the reduction in risk (fatalities per year) was also developed for the entire NCDOT Sealed Corridor for private crossings through 2010. Risk is the product of probability of a crash occurring and estimating the resulting severity of each crash. For example, if one crossing has one crash per year with one fatality and another crossing has only one crash every 10 years, but there are 10 fatalities in that crash, the statistical risk is the same at each crossing—one fatality per year. Fatalities were chosen as being an essential measure of safety without some of the ambiguity involved in injury counts or other measures.

1.5   NCDOT Corridor Activities

Using modified standard technologies, NCDOT's Rail Division ensures railroad operations are safer by closing redundant private crossings or adding additional warning devices (e.g., cross bucks, stop signs, flashing lights and gates, and gates with locking mechanisms) to the 46 remaining private crossings along the Sealed Corridor.

Table 2 shows detailed information about each of the 46 private crossings analyzed in this report, including crossing number, milepost, road name, type of treatment, and the treatment date.

The following treatment dates were assumed for this research:

- The Norfolk Southern treatments consisting of a private crossing and stop sign, as shown in Figure 4, were estimated to have been implemented, based on email communications with NCDOT, on June 10, 2005, for the 13 crossings highlighted in green in Table 2.

- The crossings with gates and locking mechanisms already in place at the time of the PCSI project original inventory (crossing numbers 734754R, 734740H, 722353G, 904230A, 722313J, and 917037B4), highlighted in blue in Table 2, were assumed to have been implemented on December 15, 2002, based on email communications with NCDOT.

- Some traffic volume data were unavailable. Volume data were based on land use, number of structures, and field observations by NCDOT.

Table 2. Phase IV Treatments Implemented through 2008

Crossing #	Milepost	Road Name	Type Crossing	Upgrade	Upgrade Date
630652H	S162.25	Recreational Vent	Private	CL	1/8/2003
630659F	163.82	Public Service Co. of NC	Private	CL	1/8/2003
630660A	164.02	First State Comm., Inc.	Private	Xbucks/stop/pvt xsign	6/10/2005
734754R	H071.11	Progress Energy	Private	G&L	12/15/2003
734751V	H067.75	Long Beverage, Inc.	Private	G&F	11/18/1997
736173A	63.98	NorthernTelecom, Inc.	Private	CL	6/15/2004
726293N	62.34	IBM, Inc. (#3)	Private	G&L	11/18/1997
736223B	61.8	Sanmina/Duke (IBM #2)	Private	CL	1/6/2004
734740H	H061.63	IBM, Inc. (#1)	Private	G&L	12/15/2002
735206G	H052.52	W. Durham Lumber Co.	Private	G&F	7/30/1994
735199Y	H048.49	5300 Old Hillsborough Rd	Private	Xbucks/stop	6/10/2005
726305F	47.62	Greenbrier Drive	Private	Xbucks/stop	6/10/2005

10

Crossing #	Milepost	Road Name	Type Crossing	Upgrade	Upgrade Date
735189T	H043.89	Byrdsville Rd	Private	G&F	10/24/2002
735160V	H041.82	Terrell's Trailer Park	Private	G&F	7/12/2005
735148N	H038.85	Frank E. Freeman & Wife	Private	Xbucks/stop	6/10/2005
735147G	H038.23	Andrew B. Lloyd & Wife	Private	Xbucks/stop	6/10/2005
736180K	28.58	Richard C. Roberts & Wife	Private	Xbucks/stop	6/10/2005
735466A	H028.21	James D. Norris & Wife	Private	Xbucks	11/18/1997
904413T	9.5	5915 Carmon Rd	Private	Xbucks	10/24/2003
722977X	H008.61	Bullard & Black	Private	Xbucks/stop	10/24/2003
722974C	H007.40	Long+Patterson	Private	Xbucks/stop	10/24/2003
722973V	H007.15	NW Tree & Stone, Co.	Private	CL	10/24/2003
722972N	H006.77	Robert Rankin Fryar	Private	Xbucks/stop	10/24/2003
722963P	H004.25	Thomas & Howard, Inc.	Private	CL	10/24/2003
722353G	295.18	Pump Station Rd	Private	G&L	12/15/2002
904230A	0303.95	206 Albertson Rd	Private	G&L	12/15/2002
722313J	0313.96	Randall T. Byerly	Private	G&L	12/15/2002
910616L	0325.20	N.C. Wildlife	Private	Xbucks/stop	6/10/2005
722196R	0327.02	Yadkin, Inc./Pittsburg, PA	Private	Xbucks/stop	6/10/2005
904231G	0328.10	NC Finishing Plant	Private	CL	7/15/2004
724363U	0336.54	Ms. W. Pat Sloop	Private	Xbucks/stop	10/28/1997
724364B	0337.06	A. & Q. Chunn	Private	G&L	10/28/1997
724366P	0337.52	Reid Farm Rd	Private	Xbucks/stop	6/10/2005
724375N	0340.61	Universal Forest Prod., Inc	Private	CL	7/30/2007
724377C	0341.39	Ethel Lane	Private	Xbucks/stop	6/10/2005
724378J	0341.54	Juke Box Rd	Private	Xbucks/stop	6/10/2005
715322R	0358.08	NS Maint. Access	Private	G&L	7/18/1994
904189K	0360.10	NS Maint. Access	Private	G&L	3/12/2008
715329N	0363.30	Ms. Gladys H. Doster	Private	Xbucks/stop	6/10/2005
917037B	0365.85	City of Charlotte	Private	G&L	12/15/2002
715335S	0366.29	Duke power Co.	Private	G&L	2/20/2003
715336Y	0336.61	H.L. Mozingo & Wife	Private	Xbucks/stop	6/10/2005
715338M	0367.00	J.B. Stroup, Jr. & Wife	Private	G&F	2/20/2002
715340N	0368.08	IP Merryhue Farms, LLC	Private	CL	1/29/2007
715344R	0369.92	8400 Old Concord Rd	Private	CL	1/29/2007
715388R	0375.64	NS Maint. Access	Private	None	NA

CL = closure; G&F = gates and flashing lights; G&L = gates with locking mechanisms; Xbucks = cross bucks

1.6   NCDOT Treatment Descriptions

Relatively few data elements are required for submission for private crossings to the USDOT inventory. Furthermore, because the data submissions were voluntary, the existing private crossing data are in many cases not accurate or up to date. Indeed, in many instances, the particular data fields reviewed were recorded as unavailable or unknown.

The data currently stored in the USDOT National Highway-Railroad Crossing Inventory for private crossings are generally not current, not suited for most analyses, and were historically not intended to support effective resource allocation. Additional data were gathered from outreach efforts by NCDOT, NCDOT's consultant partners, and railroad and private stakeholders.

1.6.1 Closure

When crossing improvements are considered, it is important to evaluate whether crossing closure or consolidation is feasible. Multiple crossings in close proximity that provide access to the same area could be considered redundant and therefore eligible for closure. The NCDOT's Rail Division considers a crossing redundant if it is within one-quarter mile of another crossing connected to the same street network (11). Figure 3 shows an example of a closure implementation.

Figure 3. View of a Sample Crossing Closure Treatment (Volpe Center)

1.6.2 Stop and Private Crossing Sign Treatment

One of the measures implemented to increase safe operations at grade railroad crossings, public and private, is upgrading the crossing warning devices, including signs, bells, and flashing signals. These are used to warn motorists, at or approaching a crossing, of an advancing train. Passive devices, which include advance warning signs, railroad cross bucks, and standard stop signs, are generally used on low-volume crossings. Active devices, including flashing lights, bells, and gates, are used on higher volume crossings with greater accident potential, or where existing conditions warrant more aggressive traffic control. Figure 4 shows a set of passive devices that include both a stop sign and a private crossing sign coupled with a "LOOK" directional sign.

Figure 4. Private Grade Crossing Stop and Cross Buck Sign Treatment (15)

1.6.3 Cross Buck Treatment

Figure 5 shows an example of a cross buck sign, which is designated as R15-1 in the MUTCD (5), at Robert Ranking Fryar Road in Guilford County, NC (crossing number 722972N).

Figure 5. Private Grade Crossing Cross Buck Sign Treatment (16)

14

1.6.4 Gates with Locking Mechanism Treatment

Highway-rail grade crossing systems consisting of gates with locking mechanisms are increasingly popular at private crossings. These installations add a locking mechanism to the conventional gated crossing. These gates block traffic on a single approach of the crossing, making it very difficult for a motorist to go around them in an attempt to violate this type of warning device. For the NCDOT Sealed Corridor, these treatments consisted of user-operated locked gates. Figure 6 shows an example of a gate with a locking mechanism installation at Davidson Co. (crossing number 904230A).

Figure 6. Private Grade Crossing Gate with Locking Mechanism Treatment (15)

1.6.5 Gates and Flashing Lights, Signs, and Pavement Marking Treatments

NCDOT's sign and pavement marking upgrades were implemented based on the condition of the existing signs and markings at crossings. Signs advising the motorist where to stop were placed on all crossings also receiving active crossing signals. Figure 7 shows such a treatment leading to IBM, Inc., Durham County (crossing number 726293N). An advance warning sign, designated as W10-1 in the MUTCD (5), and pavement markings are shown at this active crossing. Another sign placed at all crossings that receive treatment through the Sealed Corridor program provided a 1-800 emergency notification system telephone number that motorists can use to call the railroad to report any malfunctions of the crossing signals. This type of sign is designated as I-13 in the MUTCD (5).

Figure 7. Private Grade Crossing Gate, Flashing Light, and Pavement Markings Treatment (16)

2. Assessment Methods and Results

The Volpe Center conducted a site visit along the North Carolina Sealed Corridor to capture the condition of all crossings, with and without treatments. The Volpe Center also examined various databases including the FRA RAIRS, NCDOT Collision reports, police reports, and newspaper articles. Analysis on this data was performed using two different methods to estimate the number of lives saved and the potential for sustainability of a reduction in collisions through 2010. The Volpe Center team created a database with the following data field categories for each crossing: crossing ID, milepost, road name, location, county, implementation phase, public or private crossing designation, active or passive treatments, type of treatment, construction status of each treatment, and the final implementation date.

The first method used by Volpe Center was the fatal crash analysis method to calculate the differences between the annual/monthly fatality rates, based on actual experience at each of the treated crossings, before and after the improvement implementation. The before-and-after rates were calculated by determining the number of years or months that each condition was in place for each crossing in the study. The sum of these results was then calculated over all of the 46 crossings on which improvements were implemented.

The second method used was the modified USDOT APF along with severity formulas, which recognize the probabilistic nature of grade crossing fatalities and rely on a combination of actual experience at the improved crossings and an extensive database of experience at similar crossings nationwide. The formula was used to estimate the annual fatality risk at each crossing before and after each improvement.

To estimate potential future accident reduction rates, the second of the above methods was used to ensure that increases in train and vehicle exposure over time were considered. NCDOT estimates that by 2010 the vehicular traffic volume and the frequency and speed of trains will increase. The second method is capable of taking these factors into account under Full Build and No Build conditions.

2.1 Crash Analysis Method and Result

The ability to review the before-and-after conditions of highway-rail private grade crossings with fatal crashes is very useful in determining the estimated benefits of the treatment implemented. Four private grade crossings along the NCDOT corridor were specifically analyzed to assess the number of fatalities that occurred in the pretreatment conditions, and also used to determine the estimate of lives saved under the post-treatment condition through 2008. All crashes from 1990 through 2008 were considered for the fatal crash analysis, but only crossings with fatal crashes, a total of four, were selected. From 1990 to the time the treatment was implemented, a fatality rate was calculated by using the crash history for each of the crossings, assuming the warning device remained unchanged during the pretreatment period. From the time of crossing improvement through 2008, actual experience was compared with the pretreatment fatality rate to determine the potential for lives saved resulting from the treatment. A total of 26 crashes occurred on 44 private crossings within the corridor from 1990 through 2008, resulting in eight injuries and four fatalities. Table 3 shows the historical fatalities for 5 years prior to treatment of the four crossings and illustrates an average of 0.2 fatalities per year during that pretreatment period.

Table 3. Five-Year Pretreatment Fatal Crash Analysis Fatality Rate

Improvement	Crossing Name	Milepost	Historical Fatalities (5 years prior to treatment)
CL	8400 Old Concord Rd.	036992	0
Gates/Flashing Lights	Byrdsville Rd.	H04389	0
CL	IP Merryhue Farms LLC	036808	1
Xbucks	NW Tree & Stone Co.	H00715	0
Average Fatalities per year			**0.2**

CL = closure; Xbucks = cross bucks

The fatal crash rate analysis for each of these four crossings is shown in Table 4 and Figure 8. Table 4 shows the distribution of that rate over the post-treatment time period to obtain the number of estimated lives saved. The fatality rate was calculated by dividing the number of pretreatment fatalities for each crossing dating back to 1990 by the number of months within the pretreatment time period. The fatal crash rate for each crossing was then multiplied by the post-treatment time period. Any post-treatment fatalities were subtracted from the estimated lives saved. The final calculation determined the estimated lives saved through 2008 for each crossing.

18

Table 4. Fatal Crash Analysis Results-Estimated Lives Saved through 2008

Improvement	Crossing Name	Pretreatment		Post-treatment		Analysis of Lives Saved
		Fatalities	Timeframe (months)	Fatalities	Timeframe (months)	
CL	8400 Old Concord Rd.	1	193	0	30	0.155
Gate/Flashing Lights	Byrdsville Rd.	1	142	0	82	0.577
CL	IP Merryhue Farms LLC	1	193	0	30	0.155
Cross bucks	NW Tree & Stone Co.	1	154	0	94	0.610
	Total	4		0		1.499

CL = closure

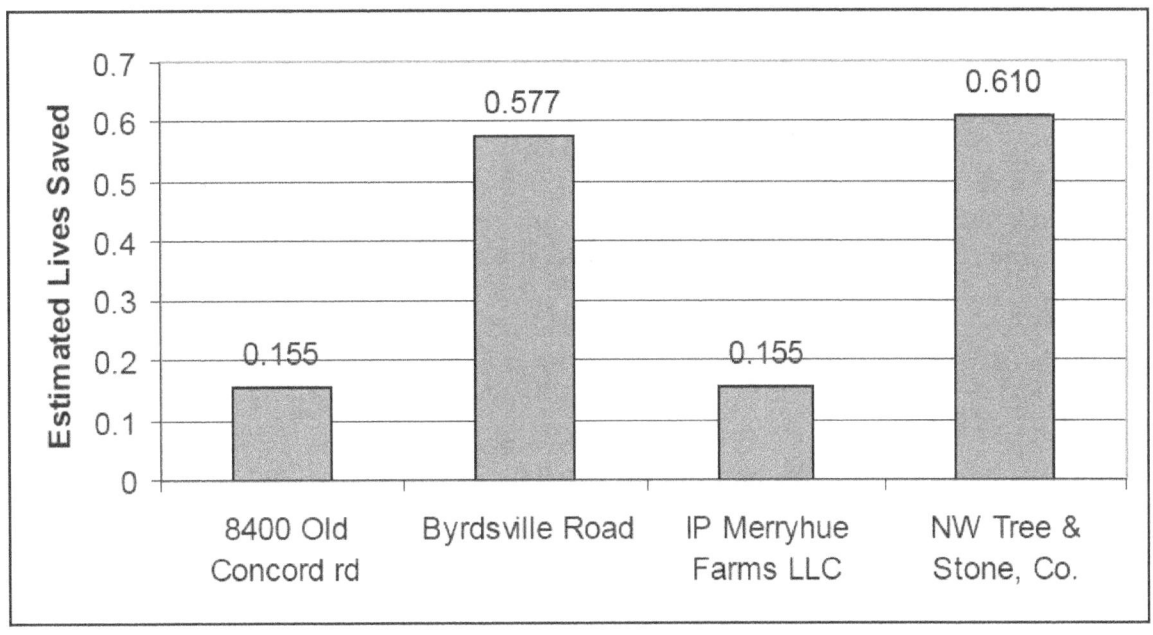

Figure 8. Fatal Crash Analysis of Estimated Lives Saved through 2008

2.2 USDOT Modified Fatal Accident Prediction Method and Results

The USDOT Fatal APF was used as the baseline to calculate risk in the corridor. This standard formula, developed by Volpe Center, has many variables to predict the severity of a crash at a grade crossing and the resulting consequences. The formula handles high-speed rail and additional enhancements and is based on the USDOT APF with updates to the collision severity portion (10–12). To determine accident probability, the study used the standard USDOT APF weighted with actual crash history. To obtain accident rate estimates for improved crossings, an effectiveness rate was applied to the baseline accident prediction result. To differentiate between freight and passenger train operations and to account for higher train speeds, the severity calculation from the APF was not used. Instead, the independent severity model described in the Empire Corridor Risk Assessment Study, which estimates risk at both public and private crossings, was used (12). This severity model incorporates vehicle mix in the determination of severity in passenger train operations.

A few data fields within the model used crossing characteristics obtained from the USDOT Inventory (7) and NCDOT rail division's inventory files such as number of tracks, number of train movements, and types of crossing warning devices. Other variables used FRA Highway-Rail Grade Crossing Accident/Incident Reports for crossing crash history. Individual crossing information was used to help determine the final risk at each crossing.

The APF is dominated by the exposure index term that combines the average daily traffic count and the number of trains. Risk is the product of the estimated probability of an event occurring based on incident history and the estimated severity of the event based on the warning type effectiveness factors. Probability is defined as the predicted number of crashes per year along a set of grade crossings. Severity is defined in this report in terms of fatalities per collision, either to train or motor vehicle occupants. Risk is presented as the number of predicted fatalities per year at the set of crossings.

The crash history factor is the collision history of the crossing over the previous 5 years. Many states regularly use the APF to help prioritize grade crossings for improvements. The validity of the APF is dependent on the previous 5-year collision history. Changes in crossing characteristics can affect the result of the modeled prediction, so the most accurate data available are used. The Rail-Highway Crossing Resource Allocation Procedure User's Guide (10) suggests that data older than 5 years could be misleading because of physical changes that may have occurred at the crossing. Therefore, each year's calculated risk is influenced by only the past 5 years of crash history. The risk is a weighted average of the crossing characteristics and the historical crashes at the crossing. This factor adjusts the final probability of a fatal crash based on historical collision information at the crossing.

2.2.1 Framework of the Risk Analysis Formula

The original DOT formula was developed based on national collision statistics from 1975 to 1980. Once the methodology was developed, current collision statistics were periodically used to upgrade various constants in the formula. This formula was developed to provide a relative risk ranking for a set of crossings and was not intended to directly compare to actual historical crash or fatality experiences, especially under conditions of small data sets.

The formula does not expressly address all of the factors that contribute to crashes. All data used for this study, including train operations, traffic growth, and timetable speeds, were obtained from FRA and NCDOT inventory databases. The national normalizing constants, which are APF factors periodically adjusted to match with the current accident and grade crossing trends, were determined by the latest collision statistics for the three types of warning devices shown in Table 5. The rationale for using this set of constants was to keep it consistent with other NCDOT reports on Phase I – III on the Sealed Corridor.

Table 5. Risk Analysis Normalizing Constants

Warning Device Groups	Normalizing Constants*
Passive	0.8239
Flashing Lights	0.6935
Gates	0.6714

*Carroll, A. *North Carolina "Sealed Corridor" Phase I: U.S. DOT Assessment Report*. Report to Congress. August 2001. www.bytrain.org/SAFETY/sealed/pdf/esvolpe.pdf, retrieved August 27, 2008. (8)

Vehicle type mix at the crossings was another factor in determining the probability of a fatal crash. The vehicle mix is used in the modified USDOT formula in the severity calculations. Once the risk is calculated using the formula, a reduction factor is applied to the final results depending on the type of treatments or improvements applied above the standard gates and flashing lights.

A modified APF, as described earlier in this chapter, was used to predict the future fatalities of the treated crossings through 2010. To be consistent with the fatal crash analysis, the modified APF estimated the risk for 5-year intervals for both pre- and post-treatment time periods. The model was populated with year-by-year input variables from both the FRA inventory and NCDOT rail division data. The model then calculated the effect of the 5-year actual incident history for prediction of future incidents.

A 2 percent per year growth in Annual Average Daily Traffic (AADT) and train frequency was assumed in the model after 2008, and train speeds were assumed to increase to 110 mph for 2010 only.

The following assumptions were used to estimate each crossing's risk:

- The effectiveness of crossings without any treatment was assumed to be zero.

- Based on the most current literature, stop sign treatments were estimated to have an effectiveness of 35 percent over passive crossings (14).

- Gates with locking mechanisms were assumed to be as effective as a standard two-quadrant gate system, which is 78 percent more effective than passive crossing treatments [10].

- Crossing closure was assumed to have an effectiveness of 100 percent over passive crossings; the risk at a closed crossing was reduced to zero.

2.2.2 Risk Formula Result with Fatal Incidents

The risk-based fatalities for the pretreatment condition were calculated for the four private grade crossings analyzed with fatal crash histories. The pretreatment risk in fatalities was determined by summing the annual risk for the 5 years before the date of the grade crossing treatment implementation, which could date back to as early as 1985 if a particular improvement was done in 1990. As shown in Table 6, the risk-based methodology calculated the total number of fatalities in the 5-year pretreatment condition to be 0.68 fatalities or a rate of 0.14 fatalities per year.

Table 6. Risk-Based Predicted Lives Lost under Pretreatment Conditions

Improvement	Crossing Name	Mile Post	Pretreatment Risk (Fatalities/5 yrs)
CL	8400 Old Concord Road	036992	0.28
Gate/Flashing Lights	Byrdsville Road	H04389	0.24
CL	IP Merryhue Farms LLC	036808	0.07
Xbucks	NW Tree & Stone, Co.	H00715	0.09
Total 5 yr Pretreatment Fatalities			**0.68**
Total Pretreatment Fatalities/Yr			**0.14**

CL = closure; Xbucks = cross bucks

Estimates of lives saved for the same set of crossings was determined from fatal accident rate predictions. The post-treatment risk was calculated using the 5 future years from the date of the grade crossing treatment implementation. The risk-based estimate of lives saved for the post-treatment condition for the four crossings is shown in Table 7. The post-treatment risk in fatalities was determined by summing the annual risk for the 5 years after the date of the grade crossing treatment implementation. As shown in Table 7, the risk-based methodology calculated total fatalities in the 5-year post-treatment condition of 0.32, which results in a rate of 0.064 fatalities per year. The difference between the pre- and post-treatment risk is also provided in Table 7 and illustrates the estimated lives saved per year for each crossing.

As shown in Table 7, the model estimates lives saved using the risk-based 5-year before-and-after condition to be approximately 0.36 lives saved, which is equivalent to 0.07 lives saved per year. The results for both methods, the fatal crash analysis and the modified USDOT formula, have trend results indicating a reduction of risk. It should be noted that the 5 years post-treatment risk at Byrdsville Road went up after flashing lights and gates were installed due to a post-treatment injury and fatality at that crossing.

**Table 7. Predicted Lives Saved for Treated Crossings over the
Post-treatment 5-Year Period**

Improvement	Crossing Name	Pretreatment Risk (Fatalities/ 5 yrs)	Post-treatment Risk (Fatalities/ 5 yrs)	Predicted "Lives Saved" for 5 yrs after Treatment
CL	8400 Old Concord Road	0.28	0.00	0.28
Gate/Flashing Lights	Byrdsville Road	0.24	0.25	-0.01
CL	IP Merryhue Farms LLC	0.07	0.00	0.07
Xbucks	NW Tree & Stone, Co.	0.09	0.07	0.02
		0.68	**0.32**	
Predicted Average 5 Yr "Lives Saved"				**0.36**
Predicted Average "Lives Saved"/Yr				**0.07**

CL = closure; Xbucks = cross bucks

2.2.3 Total Private Crossings Risk Formula Result

Figure 9 compares the overall risk at the 46 private crossings along the NCDOT corridor between 1991, before any type of treatment was in place for any of the private crossings, and 2008, after 44 of the 46 private crossings had been treated. The results show that between 1991 and 2008 the risk at the private crossings along the corridor was reduced by 57.7 percent, from 0.681 fatalities per year in 1991 to 0.288 fatalities per year in 2008. This equates to an estimated 0.39 lives saved per year. Had all 46 private crossings been treated by 2008, the risk would have been reduced by an additional 1.3 percent. No adjustments for vehicular traffic or train frequency and speed were made in this portion of the analysis.

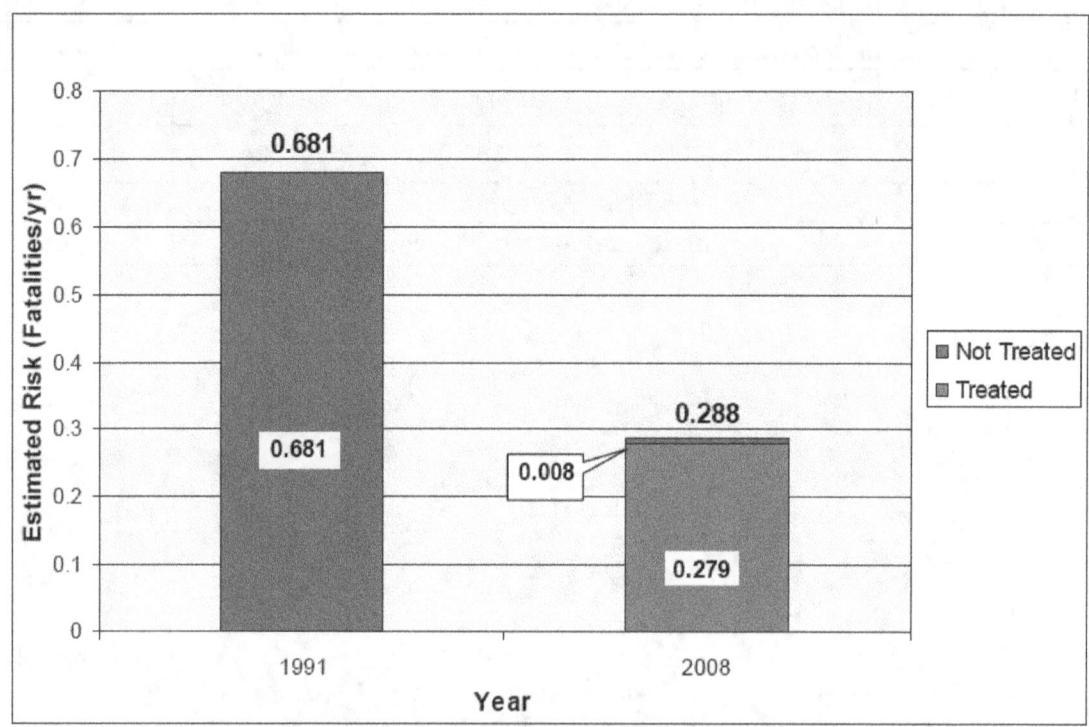

Figure 9. Estimated Risk at the 46 Private Crossings along the NCDOT Corridor

2.2.4 Estimated NCDOT Private Crossing Risk Formula Result

Figure 10 shows the estimated risk at the 46 private crossings along the NCDOT corridor in 1991 before any treatments were implemented, in 2008 after 44 of the 46 crossings were treated, and in 2010 when train speeds are assumed to increase to 110 mph, using the USDOT modified APF. The total estimated 2010 risk for both highway vehicle and train occupants is 0.36 fatalities per year. The figure also indicates that the greatest proportion of this risk, 0.33 fatalities per year, is to highway vehicle occupants. The risk of fatality to highway occupants from 1991 to 2008 has decreased by a substantial 59 percent, from 0.63 to 0.26 fatalities per year. From 1991 to 2010, with increases in vehicle and train traffic and speed, the risk is still estimated to have decreased by 47 percent, decreasing from 0.68 to 0.36 fatalities per year.

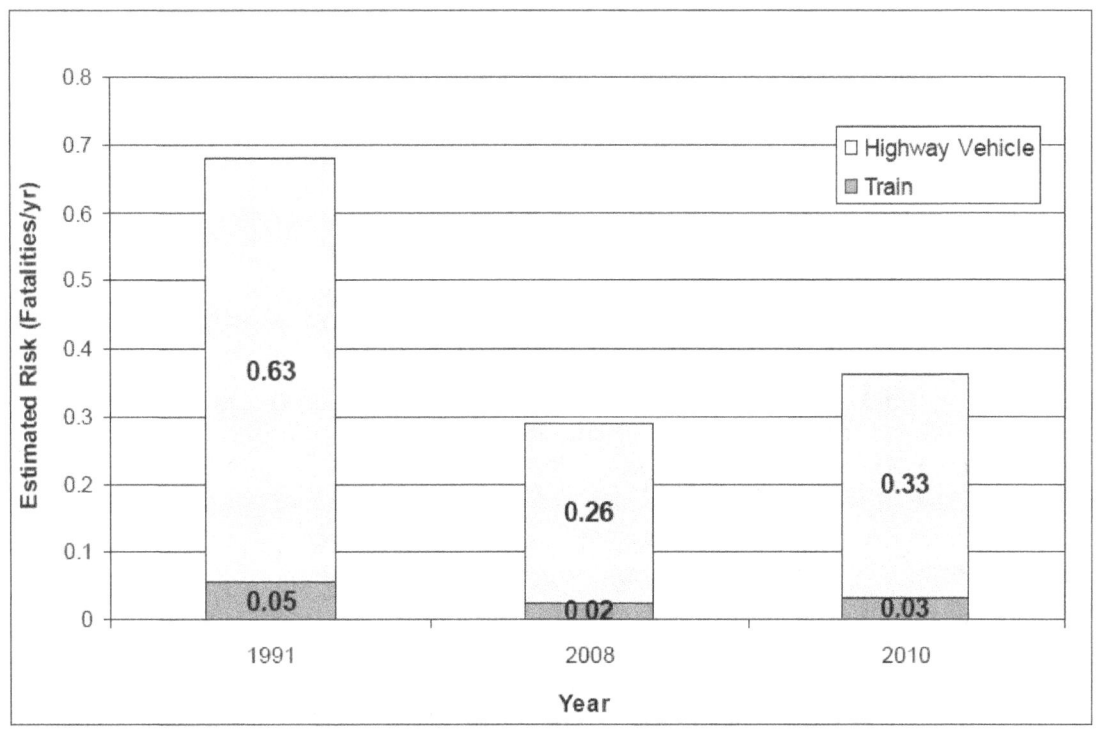

Figure 10. Estimated Risk by Vehicle Type at the 46 Private Crossings along the NCDOT Corridor

2.2.5 1990–2010 Private Crossing Results by Implementation Status

The estimated risk determined for a set of conditions was dependent on whether treatments were implemented and whether train speeds were increased to 79 or 110 mph in 2010. These conditions were:

- No Build (79 in 2010): no treatments were implemented on the 46 private crossings, but there was a 2-percent train frequency and AADT increase in 2009, and speed increased to 79 mph in 2010.
- No Build (110 in 2010): no treatments were implemented on the 46 private crossings, but there was a 2-percent train frequency and AADT increase in 2009, and speed increased to 110 mph in 2010.
- Full Build (79 in 2010): all treatments were implemented on the 46 private crossings with a 2-percent train frequency; AADT increased in 2009 and speed increased to 79 mph in 2010.
- Full Build (110 in 2010): all treatments were implemented on the 46 private crossings with a 2-percent train frequency; AADT increased in 2009 and speed increased to 110 mph in 2010.
- Full Build No Speed Increase: all treatments were implemented on the 46 private crossings with a 2-percent train frequency; AADT increased in 2009, but no increase in train speed.

The Full Build conditions assumed all of the crossing treatments and enhancements were implemented as planned on the 46 private crossings. To estimate each crossing's risk factor in 2009 and 2010 under the Full Build conditions, the condition of the corridor in 2008 was estimated through 2010 after application of modest growth factors. Since information about future trends and collision statistics were not available, certain assumptions were made. Year 2008 train volumes in the corridor were assumed to grow by 2 percent per year through 2010, and the train operating speed for 2010 for the corridor was assumed to increase to 79 and 110 mph, respectively. The AADT was assumed to grow by a factor of 2 percent per year from 2009 through 2010, and the Full Build conditions assumed a 2009 implementation date for the remaining grade crossing safety improvements. Closed private crossings had zero AADT growth applied. For collisions, the 2008 collision data were applied as a constant to the 2010 scenario. In 2010, two main tracks were used for the entire corridor as estimated by the NCDOT rail division.

For the No Build conditions, the pre-implementation crossing warning devices were assumed to remain constant and in place through 2010, meaning no treatments or enhancements were applied to the crossing. These conditions used pre-implementation AADT values with a 2-percent growth factor applied through 2010, and train speed for 2010 was assumed to increase to 79 and 110 mph, respectively. The number of train movements was increased by 2 percent annually from 2008 to 2010. For collision data, the last pre-implementation collision rate was used.

Figure 11 shows the estimated risk reduction through the year 2010 for the following two conditions, both of which include an estimated train speed increase to 110 mph in 2010:

26

- No Build (110 mph in 2010)
- Full Build (110 mph in 2010)

As shown in Figure 11, the estimated risk at those private crossings in 2010 would be about 0.79 fatalities per year under the No Build (110 mph in 2010) condition. The estimated risk would be much lower under the Full Build (110 mph in 2010) condition, estimated to be about 0.44 fatalities per year. Therefore, the estimated reduction in risk is approximately 57 percent.

Figure 12 shows the estimated risk reduction through the year 2010 for the following three conditions:

- No Build (79 mph in 2010)
- Full Build (79 mph in 2010)
- Full Build No Speed Increase

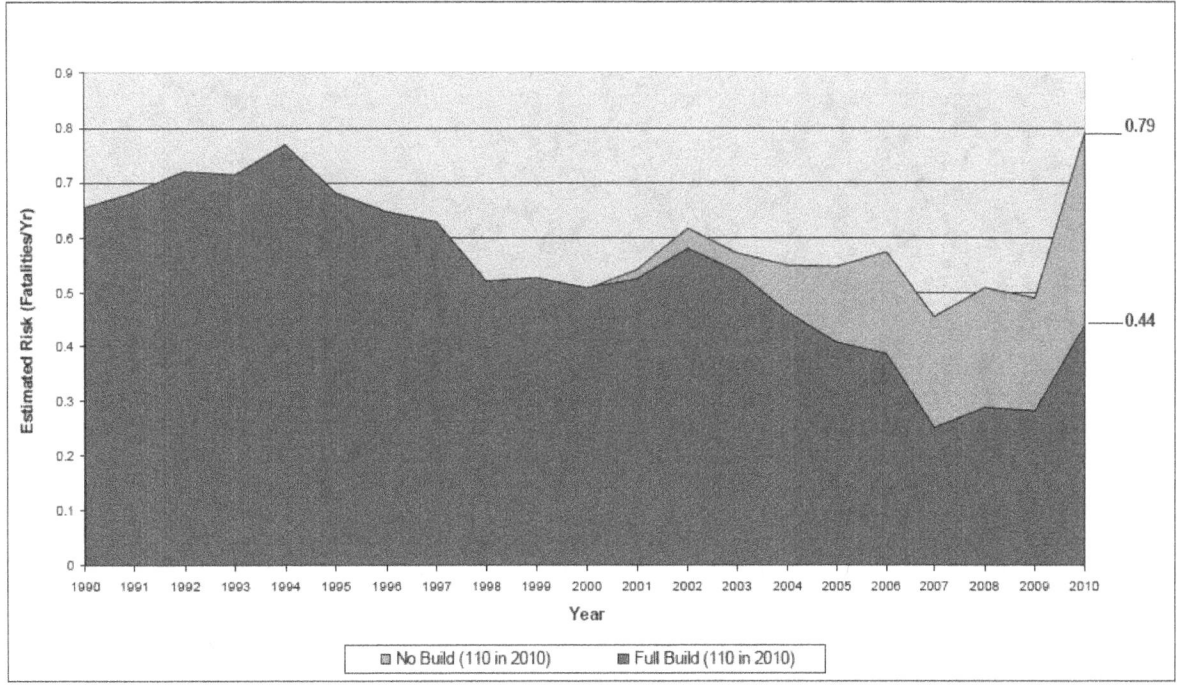

Figure 11. Estimated Risk with Higher Train Speed at the 46 Private Crossings along the NCDOT Corridor

As shown in Figure 12, the estimated risk in 2010 would be approximately 0.63 fatalities per year under the No Build (79 mph in 2010) condition. The estimated risk would be much lower under the Full Build (79 mph in 2010) condition, estimated to be about 0.36 fatalities per year. In addition, if there were no train speed increase and all of the treatments were implemented at the private crossings, denoted as the Full Build No Speed Increase condition, the estimated risk at those private crossings would be approximately 0.31 fatalities per year.

27

Table 8 summarizes the estimated risk in terms of fatalities per year at the 46 private crossings in 2010 under all five conditions. With the assumption of train speed increases to 110 mph in the year 2010, the No Build (without the application of enhanced grade crossing devices) condition shows an increase in risk per year more than the Full Build (all treated crossings) condition (0.79 versus 0.44), an estimated 56 percent reduction. If speeds were increased to only 79 mph, the No Build condition shows an increase in risk per year more than the Full Build condition (0.63 versus 0.36), an estimated 57 percent reduction.

By 2010, the fatality rate resulting from the full implementation of improvements to the entire Sealed Corridor would be 44 percent lower than if no implementation were completed and train speed increased to 110 mph. The fatality rate would be 42.8 percent lower if the speeds increased to only 79 mph in 2010, and 42 percent lower with no increase in speed in 2010.

This risk assessment, therefore, illustrates that the treatments and private crossing enhancements made in the Sealed Corridor program have resulted in a benefit in terms of lives saved through 2010 and will save even more lives for years thereafter.

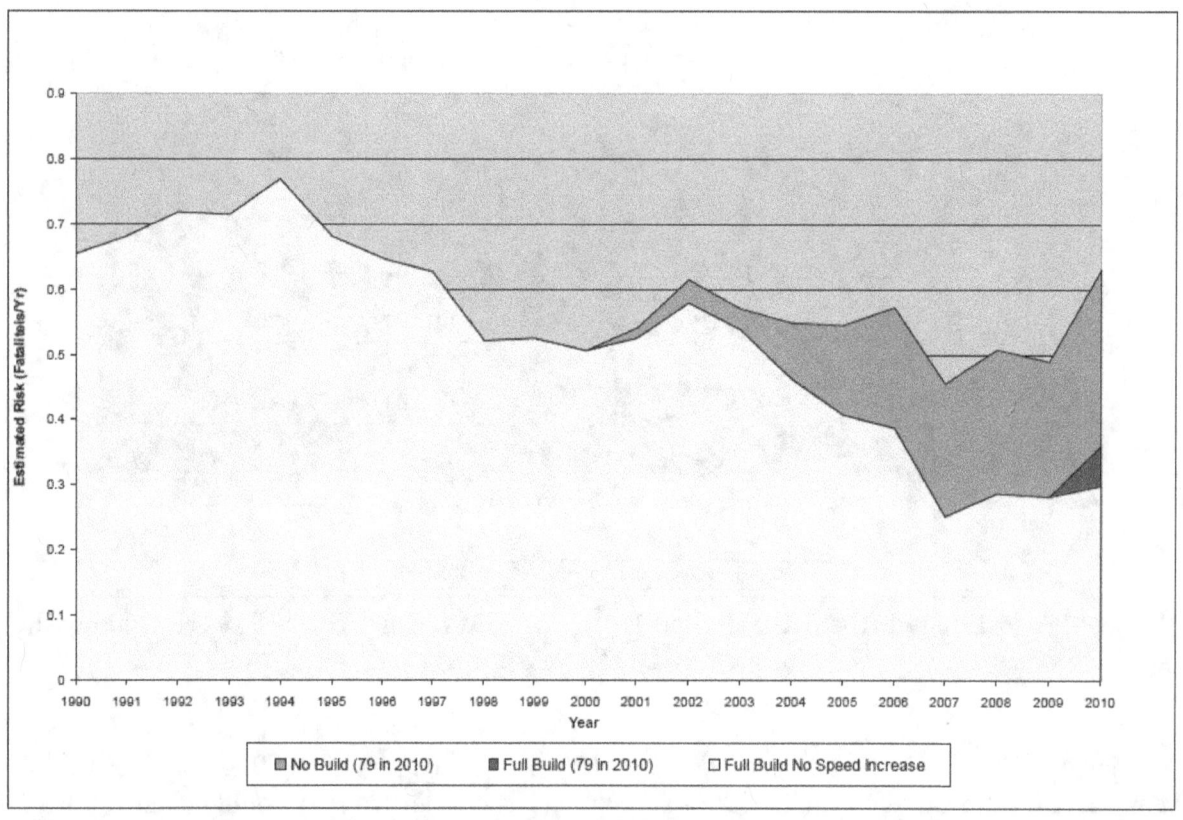

Figure 12. Estimated Risk at 79 Miles per Hour Train Speed at the 46 Private Crossings along the NCDOT Corridor

Table 8. Estimated Risk (fatalities/year) at the 46 Private Crossings in 2010

Condition	Speed Regimes		
	79 mph in 2010	110 mph in 2010	No Speed Increase
No Build	0.63	0.79	
Full Build	0.36	0.44	0.31

3. Total Sealed Corridor Public and Private Results

3.1   Phases I, II, and III Public Crossings Results

The entire NCDOT Sealed Corridor public crossings enhancement project covered a total of 208 crossings, 189 of which had been treated and 19 of which were in the process of being treated at the time of this report. An assessment of the implemented improvements at these crossings was conducted by Volpe Center and contained in the FRA Final Report entitled *North Carolina "Sealed Corridor" Phase I, II, and III Assessment* (9).

There were 282 crashes for all of the Phases I, II, and III public crossings from 1987, which was the earliest year used for the assessment conducted through 2004 in the Phase I–III Volpe study. A total of 33 grade crossings with fatal crashes were analyzed to assess the number of fatalities that occurred in the pretreatment conditions and to estimate lives saved under the post-treatment condition through 2004. The results yielded an estimated 19 lives saved as a result of the 189 improvements implemented through September 2004. The risk-based fatalities for the pretreatment condition were calculated for the 33 grade crossings analyzed with fatal crash histories. The pretreatment risk in fatalities was determined by summing the annual risk for the 5 years before the date of the grade crossing treatment, which included the previously stated timeframe, 1987. The risk-based methodology calculated the total number of fatalities in the 5-year pretreatment condition to be 4.07 fatalities, or a rate of 0.81 fatalities per year.

The estimated lives saved for the same set of crossings was determined from the USDOT APF predictions. The post-treatment risk was calculated using the 5 future years from the date of the grade crossing improvement. The post-treatment risk in fatalities was determined by summing the annual risk for the 5 years after the date of the grade crossing treatment. The risk-based methodology calculated the total number of fatalities in the 5-year post-treatment condition to be 1.94, or a rate of 0.39 fatalities per year. The calculated lives saved using the risk-based 5-year before-and-after conditions indicated that approximately two lives have been saved. Therefore, the estimated rate of lives saved is equivalent to 0.43 lives per year. The results for both methods, the fatal crash analysis and the modified USDOT APF formula, have trend results indicating a reduction of risk.

Phase I, II, and III risk for 1991 (under the No Build condition) and 2004 for the 189 treated crossings plus the 19 untreated crossings were compared. The results showed that between 1991 and 2004 the estimated risk for the treated crossings was reduced by 50.9 percent or about two lives saved per year. The estimated risk along the entire corridor under Phases I–III, had all of the improvements been completed by September 2004, would have been reduced by 57.3 percent for the same time period. The estimated 2010 risk for Phases I, II, and III was 2.3 fatalities per year. The risk to highway occupants from 1991 to 2004 decreased by a substantial 51 percent, and was estimated to decrease 43 percent from 1991 to 2010 even with increases in vehicle and train traffic.

3.2   Phase IV Private Crossings Results

The NCDOT Sealed Corridor Private Crossings project covered a total of 46 crossings, 44 of which had been treated and 2 of which were in the process of being treated at the time of this report. There were a total of 26 crashes across all of the 46 private crossings included in Phase IV from 1985 through 2008. A total of four grade crossings with fatal crashes were analyzed to assess the number of fatalities that occurred in the pretreatment conditions and to estimate the number of potential lives saved under the post-treatment condition through 2008. The results yielded an estimate of 1.5 lives saved as a result of the 44 improvements implemented through September 2008. The risk-based fatalities for the pretreatment condition were calculated for the four grade crossings analyzed with fatal crash histories. The pretreatment risk in fatalities was determined by summing the annual risk for the 5 years before the date of the grade crossing treatment. The risk-based methodology calculated the total number of fatalities in the 5-year pretreatment condition to 0.68 fatalities, or a rate of 0.14 fatalities per year.

The estimated number of lives saved for the same set of crossings was determined from USDOT-modified APF predictions. The post-treatment risk was calculated using the 5 future years from the date of the grade crossing improvement. The post-treatment risk in fatalities was determined by summing the annual risk for the 5 years after the date of the grade crossing treatment. The risk-based methodology calculated the total number of fatalities in the 5-year post-treatment condition to be 0.32, or a rate of 0.064 fatalities per year. The calculated lives saved using the risk-based 5-year before-and-after conditions indicated that approximately 0.36 lives have been saved. Therefore, the estimated rate of lives saved is equivalent to 0.07 lives per year. The results for both methods, the fatal crash analysis and the modified USDOT formula, have trend results indicating a reduction of risk.

Phase IV risk for 1991, before any treatments were implemented, and 2008, after 44 of the 46 private crossings had been treated, were compared. The results showed that between 1991 and 2008 the risk for the treated crossings was reduced by 57.7 percent, or 0.39 lives saved per year. The entire corridor Phase IV risk, had it been completed by September 2008, would have been reduced by 59 percent for the same time period. The estimated 2010 risk for Phase IV was estimated to be 0.36 fatalities per year. The risk to highway occupants from 1991 to 2008 decreased by a substantial 59 percent and was estimated to decrease 47 percent from 1991 to 2010 even with increases in vehicle and train traffic.

3.3   Phases I–III (Public Crossings) and Phase IV (Private Crossings) Results

The entire NCDOT Sealed Corridor project covered a total of 254 public and private crossings, 233 of which had been treated and 21 of which are in the process of being treated. There were 308 crashes for the entire corridor from 1987 through 2008. A total of 37 grade crossings with fatal crashes were analyzed to assess the number of fatalities that occurred in the pretreatment conditions and to estimate the potential number of lives saved under the post-treatment condition through September 2008. The results yielded an estimate of 21 lives saved as a result of the 233 improvements implemented through September 2008 in all public and private crossings in the NCDOT corridor.

Figure 13 shows the estimated risk through 2010 on the entire NCDOT corridor, including public crossings, which were treated during Phases I–III of the program, for the same five conditions defined above in Subsection 2.2.5.

31

With the assumption of speed increase to 110 mph in 2010, the No Build condition shows more of an increase in risk per year in 2010 than the Full Build condition (6.09 versus 2.93). If speeds were increased to only 79 mph, the No Build condition shows more of an increase in risk per year than the Full Build (5.44 versus 2.67). Further analysis of the No Build condition indicates an increase of 1.8 fatalities per year more than the 2010 Full Build condition if there were no speed increase. By 2010, the fatality rate resulting from the full implementation of all of the public and private crossing treatments along the entire NCDOT corridor would be 52 percent lower than if no implementation were executed and the train speed increased to 110 mph. The fatality rate would be 50.9 percent lower if the train speeds increased to only 79 mph in 2010, and 46 percent lower with no increase in train speed in 2010. This risk assessment, therefore, illustrates that the treatments and all public and private crossing enhancements made in the NCDOT Sealed Corridor program have resulted in additional benefits in terms of lives saved through 2010, and will save even more lives for years thereafter.

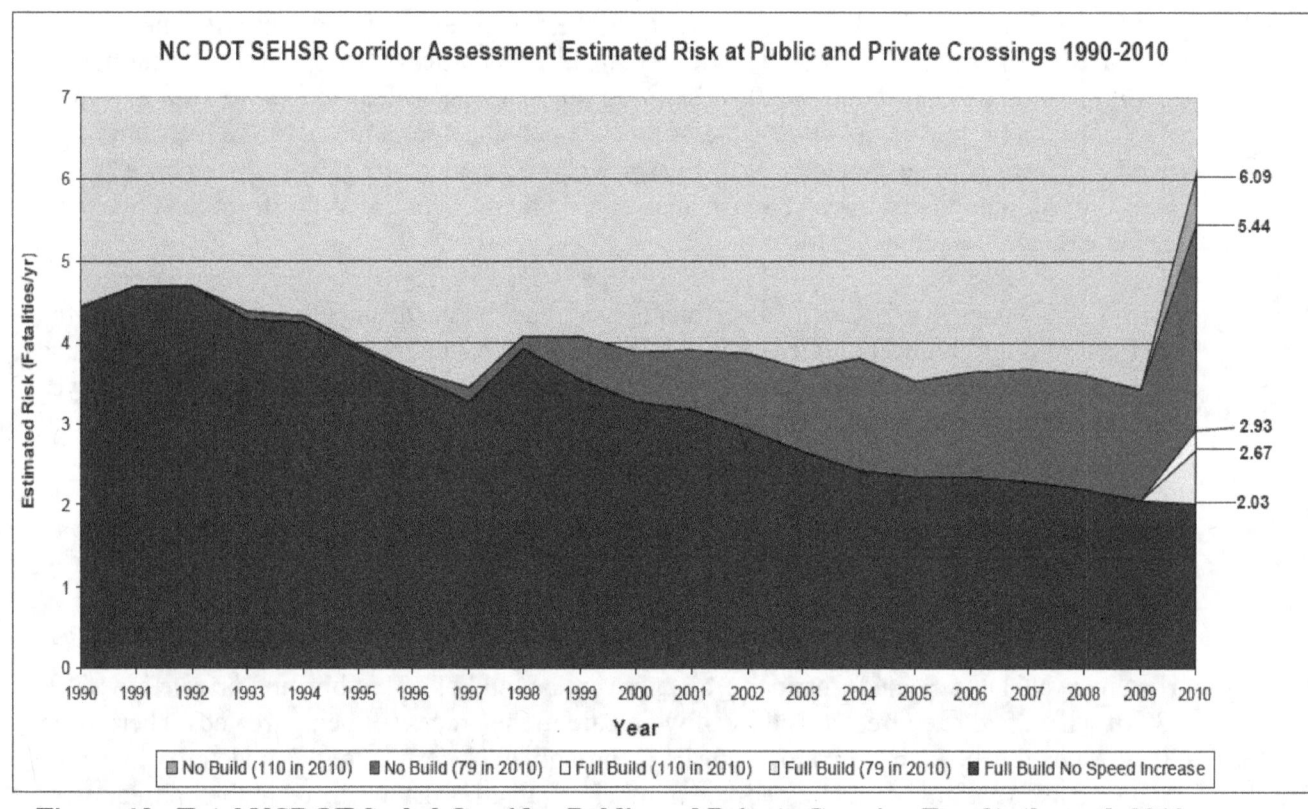

Figure 13. Total NCDOT Sealed Corridor Public and Private Crossing Results through 2010

4. Findings

The objective of this research was to assess the potential benefits provided by the safety improvements at private highway-rail grade crossings in North Carolina along the Charlotte to Raleigh portion of the SEHSR. The NCDOT proceeded with this set of safety improvements, commonly grouped under the PCSI program, under Phase IV of their Sealed Corridor program.

The PCSI encompasses 46 private crossings between Charlotte and Raleigh, NC. As of September 2008, a total of 44 of the 46 crossings had been improved or closed. The research documented in this report calculates the estimated number of lives saved based on the improvements made to these highway-rail intersections from 1990 through September 2008. The results of this research provide a substantive analysis of the Sealed Corridor private crossing implementation and provide Federal, State, and local organizations a successful model to utilize on their high-speed rail corridors.

4.1 Findings Summary

The NCDOT Sealed Corridor PCSI encompasses 46 private crossings, 44 of which have been upgraded and 2 of which are being upgraded at the time of this report. Before the project started, most of the crossings were passive. The most employed method of treatment was cross bucks with a stop sign, which were used at 18 crossings. Gates with locking mechanisms were installed at 11 crossings, gates with flashing lights were installed at 5 crossings, cross bucks were set up at 3 crossings, and 8 crossings were closed.

The following assumptions were made for this research:

- The Norfolk Southern treatment consisting of a private crossing sign and stop sign, as shown in Figure 4, was estimated to have been implemented, based on email communication with NCDOT, on 6/10/2005 for the thirteen crossings highlighted in bright green in Table 2.

- The crossings with gates and locks already in place at the time of PCSI project's original inventory (crossing number 734754R, 734740H, 722353G, 904230A, 722313J, and 917037B4) highlighted in blue in Table 2 were assumed to have been implemented in December 15, 2002, based on email communications with NCDOT.

- Some traffic volume data were unavailable. Volume data was based upon land use, number of structures, and field observations by NCDOT.

Some residential crossings serve multiple properties: the one at Byrdsville Road (number 735189T) serves 67 residential units, Terrell's Trailer Park (number 735160V) provides access to 12 units, Ethel Lane (number 724377C) serves 18, and 8400 Old Concord Road (number 715344R) serves 7 residential units. The crossing at J.B. Stroup, Jr., & Wife (number 715338M) has potential to access 300 acres of undeveloped land. Twenty seven of the crossings serve one or more occupied residential structures or commercial/industrial operations.

Some industrial crossings pose special hazards: the Public Service Company of NC crossing (number 630659F) provides access to a propane storage and distribution facility, and the Robert Rankin Fryar crossing (number 722972N) provides access to a quarry and demolition landfill operations.

Private crossings typically exist as a result of an agreement between a railroad company and the property owner of record at the crossing. In some cases, written and recorded agreements exist between the two private parties. In other cases, however, the crossing may have been installed under the terms of a non-recorded agreement or installed by the owner/user without railroad permission.

Many safety treatments and initiatives have been implemented at public crossings. However, because of the characteristics of and the inherent responsibilities regarding private property, private crossings have not received many of the public grade crossing treatments and initiatives.

Private highway-rail grade crossings may be governed by legal agreements between private property owners and private railroad companies. Currently, few Federal regulations pertain to the safety, operation, maintenance, or responsibility designations at private highway-rail grade crossings, though some States and local jurisdictions have assumed varying degrees of authority over them.

4.2   Conclusions and Recommendations

This report documents the benefits of North Carolina's Sealed Corridor program at highway-rail private grade crossings. The specific route encompassing the Sealed Corridor consists of 173.3 miles of Norfolk Southern track that runs through Raleigh – Cary – Durham – Hillsborough – Burlington – Greensboro – High Point – Salisbury – Kannapolis – and Charlotte.

The total NCDOT Sealed Corridor includes 254 crossings, 208 of which are public crossings and 46 of which are private crossings. This report assesses Phase IV of the Sealed Corridor program, which aimed at improving or closing private crossings on the rail lines that run between Charlotte and Greensboro with predictions for future reductions in fatalities through 2010. Several types of grade crossing treatments to reduce the risk of fatality were investigated by NCDOT. These grade crossing improvements included cross bucks, flashing lights and gates, signals, and locking gates.

The North Carolina Sealed Corridor architecture is typical of the five originally designated high-speed rail corridors nationwide. The NCDOT corridor is typically single track including sidings and approximately one crossing per mile. As of 2003 the route carries 35 freight trains per day and approximately six daily passenger trains. It has a mix of public and private crossings, the route contains both urban as well as rural environs, and the railroad operating speeds fall within the track Class 4 category. Plans for this corridor include operation at speeds up to 110 mph.

A review was conducted of the 44 treated private crossings along the Sealed Corridor. The Sealed Corridor includes 46 private crossings, but 2 crossings have not been treated at the time of this assessment. A review of the crash history for these 44 private crossings indicates 26 crashes occurred between 1985 and 2008. A total of 4 fatalities were reported for those 26 highway vehicle-train crashes. Examination of the accident reports of the four treated crossings with fatal accident histories was conducted.

A fatal crash rate was determined for each of the four crossings that had a fatal crash history from 1985 through 2008. The crash rate was distributed over the post-treatment period to obtain a value of estimated lives saved in the post-treatment period through 2008. It was determined that the safety treatments implemented at those private grade crossings have resulted in an estimated 1.5 lives saved through 2008.

At least one and half lives have been potentially saved.

The fatal crash analysis method resulted in an estimate of 1.5 lives saved as a result of the private crossing improvements implemented on the NCDOT corridor through 2008. The modified USDOT APF estimated that the improvements implemented through September 2008 are reducing fatalities by approximately 0.39 each year. The modified USDOT APF predicted approximately 50 percent more lives saved compared to the results obtained through the fatal crash analysis. This may be because the APF contains more variables and addresses the crossing environment risk.

The estimated accident reduction result is sustainable.

To estimate future accident reduction rates, the second of the above methods was used to ensure that increases in train and vehicle exposure over time were considered in the analysis. Since vehicle traffic volume and frequency and speed of trains are expected to increase, the second method was used because it is capable of taking those factors into account.

Figure 14 shows the estimated annual fatalities under the five treatment condition previously defined in Subsection 2.2.5. The Full Build conditions assumed all of the crossing treatments and enhancements were implemented as planned on the 46 private crossings. The No Build conditions assumed that the pre-implementation crossing warning devices remained in place through 2010, meaning no treatment or enhancements were applied to the crossing. Figure 14 shows a steady risk increase from 1990 to 1994, then a decrease from 1994 to 1998, and then an increase in risk with the introduction of the high-speed rail. The graph shows the influence of the improvements, which were initiated in 2002, on reducing the annual fatalities through the year 2009. The improvements at the remaining two crossings in the corridor were assumed to be implemented in 2009. The gradual increase in traffic volume and train frequency from 2008 through 2010 is expected to gradually increase annual fatalities under all conditions. Finally, the increase in train speed to 110 mph assumed to occur in 2010 would further increase all fatality rates.

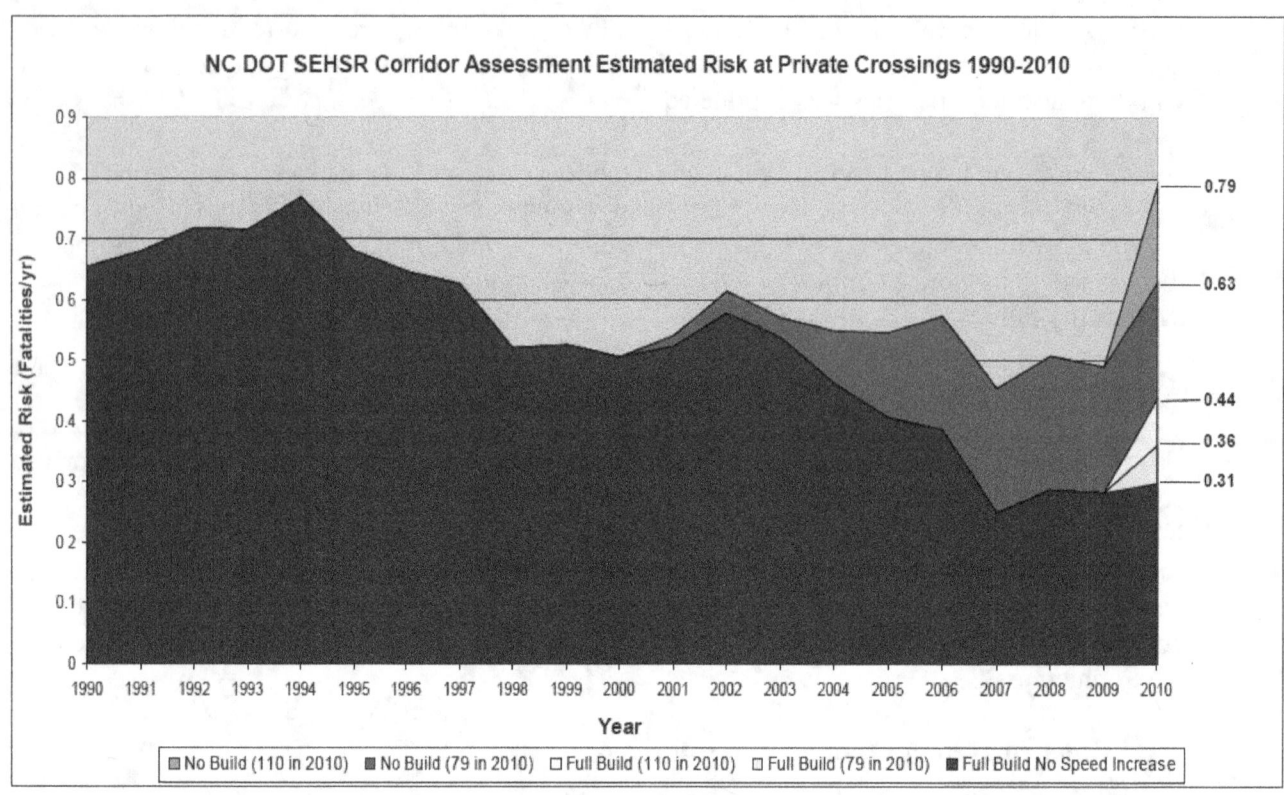

Figure 14. Estimated Risk at the 46 Private Crossings along the NCDOT Corridor through 2010

This risk assessment illustrates that the treatments and private crossing enhancements made in the Sealed Corridor program have resulted in a benefit in terms of lives saved through 2010 and will save even more lives for years thereafter. Additionally, analysis of the NCDOT project provides support for the following recommendations:

- The crossings along the NCDOT Sealed Corridor are also typical of the conditions on the 10 other high-speed rail corridors designated under Section 104 (d) (2) of Title 23 U.S. Code. This suggests that similar plans for corridor grade crossing improvements be given serious consideration with high-speed rail upgrades in these corridors.

- The implementation of the NCDOT Sealed Corridor initiative is a demonstration of nonstandard corridor highway-railroad grade crossing improvements. The NCDOT corridor should be monitored to serve as a basis for assessing the potential impact of similar programs in other corridors.

- The implementation of innovative Volpe Center research methodologies will improve additional high-speed rail corridors nationwide.

- More enhanced private crossing record keeping will increase the accuracy of data in the National Highway-Railroad Crossing Inventory.

- The safety of private crossings is a longstanding priority which the government has only recently been able to begin addressing.

5. References

(1)   U.S. Department of Transportation, Secretary of Transportation, *Rail-Highway Crossing Safety Action Plan*, Washington, DC: U.S. DOT, June 1994.

(2)   U.S. Department of Transportation, Secretary of Transportation, *Highway-Rail Crossing Safety and Trespass Prevention*, Washington, DC: U.S. DOT, June 2004.

(3)   U.S. DOT National Highway-Rail Crossing Inventory File Statistics as of 12/31/2008, compiled on February 10, 2009 (http://www.fra.dot.gov/downloads/safety/SummaryInventoryDataCounts41209.pdf, last accessed September 3, 2009).

(4)   Ogden, B., *Railroad-Highway Grade Crossing Handbook; Revised Second Edition*. Report No. FHWA-SA-07-010. U.S. Department of Transportation, Federal Highway Administration, 2007.

(5)   *Manual on Uniform Traffic Control Devices for Streets and Highways – 2003 Edition*. U.S. Department of Transportation, Federal Highway Administration, 2003. Washington, DC.

(6)   Peck, S., Carroll, A., and Kloeppel, M., *Private Highway-Rail Grade Crossing Safety Research and Inquiry* Final Report. Report No. DOT/FRA/ORD-10/02. U.S. Department of Transportation, Federal Railroad Administration, February 2010. Washington, DC.

(7)   http://safetydata.fra.dot.gov/officeofsafety/, last accessed September 10, 2009.

(8)   Carroll, A. *North Carolina "Sealed Corridor" Phase I: U.S. DOT Assessment Report*. Report to Congress. August 2001. www.bytrain.org/SAFETY/sealed/pdf/esvolpe.pdf, retrieved August 27, 2008.

(9)   Bien-Aime, P. *North Carolina "Sealed Corridor" Phase I, II, and III Assessment*. U.S. Department of Transportation, Federal Railroad Administration, Office of Research and Development, Washington, DC, DOT/FRA/ORD-09/17.

(10)   Farr, E. H. *Rail-Highway Crossing Resource Allocation Procedure: User's Guide*, 3rd ed. Report DOT-TSC-FRA-87-1. FHWA and FRA, U.S. Department of Transportation, 1987.

(11)   Worley, P., and Mastrangelo, A., "Sealed Corridor" Draft Study Results, North Carolina Department of Transportation and Norfolk Southern Corporation Report. 1997.

(12)   Mironer, M., Coltman, M., and McCown, R. *Assessment of Risks for High-Speed Rail Grade Crossings on the Empire Corridor – Next Generation High-Speed Rail Program.* FRA. Final Report August 2000. DOT-VNTSC-FRA-00-03, DOT/FRA/RDV-00/05.

(13)   49 CFR Parts 222 and 229, Use of Locomotive Horns at highway-Rail Grade Crossings; Final Rule, August 17, 2006. http://www.fra.dot.gov/downloads/safety/trainhorn_2005/amended_final_rule_081706.pdf, last accessed February 1, 2010.

(14)   National Transportation Safety Board. 1998. Safety at passive grade crossings. Volume 1: Analysis. Safety Study NTSB/SS-98/02. Washington, DC. p. 124.

(15)   Private Crossing Safety Initiative Sealed Corridor, http://www.bytrain.org/safety/sealed/private.html, last accessed September 18, 2009.

(16)   http://www.bytrain.org/safety/sealed/pdf/PSCIProjectReportOct03.pdf, last accessed February 2, 2010.

Appendix A. Estimated Risk at the 46 Private Crossings

CROSSING#	Milepost	ROADNAME	1991 Not Treated	1991 Treated	2008 Not Treated	2008 Treated
630652H	016225	Recreational Vent	0.013222			0.000000
630659F	016382	Public Service Co. of NC	0.018887			0.000000
630660A	016402	First State Comm., Inc.	0.002976			0.003493
715322R	035808	NS Maint. Access	0.005694			0.002409
715329N	036330	Ms. Gladys H. Doster	0.013441			0.007509
715335S	036629	Duke power Co.	0.005694			0.036781
715336Y	036661	H.L. Mozingo & Wife	0.009915			0.005648
715338M	036700	J.B. Stroup, Jr. & Wife	0.009915			0.007035
715340N	036808	IP Merryhue Farms, LLC	0.010964			0.000000
715344R	036992	8400 Old Concord Rd	0.018458			0.000000
715388R	037564	NS Maint. Access	0.000481		0.000481	
722196R	032702	Yadkin, Inc./Pittsburg, PA	0.003587			0.002364
722313J	031396	Randall T. Byerly	0.050193			0.005680
722353G	029518	Pump Station Rd	0.006909			0.031335
722963P	H425	Thomas & Howard Inc.	0.031345			0.018580
722972N	H677	Robert Rankin Fryar	0.011204			0.029911
722973V	H715	NW Tree & Stone, Co.	0.017970			0.014806
722974C	H00740	Long+Patterson	0.007315			0.004009
722977X	H00861	Bullard & Black	0.027742			0.003393
724363U	033654	Ms. W. Pat Sloop	0.009149		0.007538	
724364B	033706	A. & Q. Chunn	0.003854			0.002150
724366P	033752	Reid Farm Road	0.007538			0.005095
724375N	034061	Universal Forest Prod, Inc	0.028419			0.000000
724377C	034139	Ethel Lane	0.014970			0.008555
724378J	034154	Juke Box Road	0.005111			0.003411
726293N	006234	IBM Inc. (#3)	0.002575			0.002575
726305F	004762	Greenbrier Drive	0.006156			0.004154
734740H	H06163	IBM Inc. (#1)	0.008726			0.006509
734751V	H06775	Long Beverage, Inc.	0.087705			0.008707
734754R	H07111	Progress Energy	0.007601			0.004824
735147G	H03823	Andrew B. Lloyd & Wife	0.007306			0.004882
735148N	H03885	Frank E. Freeman & Wife	0.005327			0.003533
735160V	H4182	Terrell's Trailer Park	0.099951			0.005414
735189T	H4389	Byrdsville Road	0.022132			0.007812
735199Y	H04849	5300 Old Hillsborough Rd	0.009264			0.006538
735206G	H5252	W. Durham Lumber Co.	0.021695			0.007763
735466A	H02821	James D. Norris & Wife	0.008868			0.007306
736173A	006398	NorthernTelecom Inc.	0.011737			0.000000
736180K	002858	Richard C. Roberts & Wife	0.006465			0.003533
736223B	006180	Sanmina/Duke (IBM #2)	0.004323			0.000000
904189K	036010	NS Maint. Access	0.005694			0.002787
904230A	030395	206 Albertson Road	0.004750			0.002373
904231G	032810	206 Albertson Road	0.014003			0.000000
904413T	000950	5915 Carmon Rd	0.004960			0.004086
910616L	032520	N.C. Wildlife	0.004353			0.002364
917037B	036585	City of Charlote	0.002409			0.002409
Total Estimated Risk			0.680951	0.000000	0.008019	0.279733

Abbreviations and Acronyms

AADT	Annual Average Daily Traffic
APF	Accident Prediction Formula
CL	Closure
FHWA	Federal Highway Administration
FRA	Federal Railroad Administration
G&F	gates and flashing lights
G&L	gates with locking mechanisms
HSGT	High-Speed Ground Transportation
mph	miles per hour
MUTCD	Manual on Uniform Traffic Control Devices
NCDOT	North Carolina Department of Transportation
NTSB	National Transportation Safety Board
PCSI	Private Crossing Safety Initiative
RAIRS	Railroad Accident Incident Reporting System
RITA	Research and Innovative Technology Administration
SEHSR	Southeast High-Speed Rail
USDOT	U.S. Department of Transportation
Volpe Center	John A. Volpe National Transportation Systems Center
Xbucks	cross bucks